Brave Dogs, Gentle Dogs

Brave Dogs, Gentle Dogs

How They Guard Sheep

by Cat Urbigkit

Boyds Mills Press

To the John Arambel family

Text and photographs copyright © 2005 by Cat Urbigkit
All rights reserved

Published by Boyds Mills Press, Inc.
A Highlights Company
815 Church Street
Honesdale, Pennsylvania 18431
Printed in China

Library of Congress Cataloging-in-Publication Data

Urbigkit, Cat.
Brave dogs, gentle dogs : how they guard sheep / by Cat Urbigkit.—1st ed.
p. cm.
ISBN 1-59078-317-4 (alk. paper)
1. Sheep dogs—Juvenile literature. I. Title.

SF428.6.U74 2005
636.737—dc22

2004016855

First edition, 2005
The text is set in 15-point Wilke Roman.
Visit our Web site at www.boydsmillspress.com

10 9 8 7 6 5 4 3 2

IN WYOMING, Little Tuck watches over a flock of sheep as it grazes the high sagebrush plains. Little Tuck is a guardian dog. He belongs to a breed called Great Pyrenees, one of many breeds of guardian dogs found around the world.

Guardian dogs have been used to guard livestock for hundreds (even thousands) of years in the countries where they originated, including Turkey, Hungary, Italy, and Spain. About thirty years ago, ranchers brought these guardian dogs to the Rocky Mountains.

The dogs protect livestock from predators such as grizzly bears and gray wolves.

Ranchers used several different breeds of dogs. One breed of dog was often mated with another. Today many working guardians are these "crossbreds."

The names, colors, and hair coats vary, but all the guardian breeds have some things in common, including their large size when they grow into adulthood and their natural guardian instinct.

Guardian dogs, such as Snip here, are not used to move or herd livestock. Their only job is to stand guard, keeping predators from harming any members of their herds. The dogs receive very little training.

Instead, the dogs are raised with livestock, in a process called *socialization*. Ranchers help the process along by introducing the pups to their herds at a young age.

When guardian puppies are born, sheep's wool, called *fleece*, is placed in their bedding area to keep them warm and happy and to get them used to the smell of sheep. These dogs, named Sonny and Cher, are brother and sister.

After a few weeks of lying in wool,
the puppies go out to meet their sheep.

When a guardian puppy meets a sheep for the first time, sometimes both young animals are afraid, but friendships start very soon. (The puppies lick and smell their sheep a lot.)

Guardian pups learn that their sheep smell like the wool the pups sleep in.

Once the puppies learn that the lambs are nice, they begin to meet older sheep, which are much bigger than the lambs. This usually takes place when the pups are a few months old.

When a new lamb is born, the pups are
eager to meet the new arrival, but the ewe
stays close to supervise.

Guardian dogs become strongly attached to their sheep, just as dogs growing up in a home become attached to the people who live with them. This relationship is called *bonding*.

Bonding means a unique closeness
exists between the dog and the sheep.

The sheep trust their guardian dogs, and that trust is returned. Many of the dogs spend their entire lives with one herd of sheep and recognize that herd as being different from other herds.

Sometimes, a guardian dog that is lost will actually walk past other sheep herds while looking for its own herd.

These pups, just a few months old, are now big enough to follow the sheep around. They begin to stay out with the sheep as they graze during the day, then bed down with the herd at night.

When the pups misbehave, the sheep will even discipline them, as this ewe is doing, threatening to butt the pups when they try to bother her food.

These brave pups are on guard duty, but Mom is there just in case.

The mother dog often stays where she can see her pups, making sure they don't wander away from the herd or get into too much trouble.

Bears, mountain lions, and wolves are all a threat to sheep, but coyotes are their primary predator. Coyotes live in nearly every environment on the North American continent.

They are called "food opportunists," meaning they will eat almost any food that is available, from birds and mice to rabbits and deer. Coyotes also prey on domestic livestock, including sheep.

Ewes, or female sheep, are very attentive to their young, but they need guardian dogs to help protect their vulnerable babies. Guardian dogs protect their herds by barking, patrolling, and sometimes attacking predators that are trying to harm the sheep. Good guardians, they are always near.

During lambing, when ewes have their babies, shepherds keep a close eye on newborn lambs, and so do their guardian dogs. Guardian dogs can be born at any time of the year, but lambs are usually born in the spring.

This ewe has four lambs and needs full-time help. Guardian dogs make great baby-sitters.

As the pups grow up, they want to be with their sheep.
And guard them.
And stay with them always, keeping them safe from harm.

Author's Note

Sheep ranchers in the Rocky Mountains use six main breeds of dogs to protect their herds of domestic sheep from predators:

The Great Pyrenees *(PEER-ah-nees)* is named for the Pyrenees Mountains separating Spain and France. These are large, heavy-bodied white dogs like Little Tuck in the photo on page 5.

Anatolians *(An-ah-TOE-lee-ons)* are from Turkey and are generally more aggressive than other breeds. They are slimmer than Great Pyrenees and range in color from all white to tan bodies with black faces.

Akbash *(AUK-bahsh)* dogs are also from Turkey. The word *akbash* means "white head." This dog breed is believed to have been used as livestock guardians for about six thousand years.

Kuvasz *(KOO-vashz)* is another breed of large white guardian dog, but these dogs are from Hungary. They have a wavy double-hair coat.

Maremma *(Ma-RAY-ma)* is a breed of guardian dog from the mountains of Italy. Maremmas are large dogs that are always white or cream-colored.

Shar Planinetz *(Shar Pla-NEE-nets)* is a European breed that is believed to have originated in Yugoslavia. These are heavily built, powerful dogs with a thick hair coat that ranges from white to tan or black.

The dogs did so well at protecting flocks from predators in their native countries that the United States government and several universities worked to bring them to ranchers in the Rocky Mountains. The program was started when the United States Congress passed the Endangered Species Act, which protects certain animals, including predators such as grizzly bears and gray wolves. This law was passed around the same time that the use of poisons to kill predators on western rangelands ended. Ranchers needed a way to protect their herds from predators, but the predators had to be protected also. Guardian dogs were the answer.